The Work We Do

by David Conrad

Content and Reading Adviser: Mary Beth Fletcher, Ed.D.
Educational Consultant/Reading Specialist
The Carroll School, Lincoln, Massachusetts

Spyglass
BOOKS

COMPASS POINT BOOKS

Minneapolis, Minnesota

Compass Point Books
3722 West 50th Street, #115
Minneapolis, MN 55410

Visit Compass Point Books on the Internet at *www.compasspointbooks.com*
or e-mail your request to *custserv@compasspointbooks.com*

Photographs ©: PhotoDisc, cover; TRIP/J. Greenberg, 4; Imagestate, 5, 19; TRIP/S. Grant, 6, 8, 17;
TRIP/C. Rennie, 7; TRIP/H. Rogers, 9, 10, 11, 13, 16; Ann Ronan Picture Library, 12;
Tim Wright/Corbis, 14; Stock Montage, 15; Petting Zoo Publications/David McEwen, 18.

Project Manager: Rebecca Weber McEwen
Editor: Heidi Schoof
Photo Selectors: Rebecca Weber McEwen and Heidi Schoof
Designer: Erin Scott, SARIN creative
Illustrator: Anna-Maria Crum

Library of Congress Cataloging-in-Publication Data

Conrad, David.
  The work we do / by David Conrad.
     p. cm. — (Spyglass books)
Summary: Briefly introduces a wide variety of occupations.
Includes bibliographical references and index.
  ISBN 0-7565-0382-5 (hardcover)
  1. Vocational guidance—Juvenile literature. [1. Occupations.]
  I. Title. II. Series.
  HF5381.2 .C66 2002   602086
  331.7'02—dc21

                              2002002736

Contents

Every minute of every day, people are doing their jobs.

There are many different kinds of jobs. Teaching is a job. Cooking is a job. Driving a bus is a job.

Did You Know?

Staying home to take care of children is a job.

Some people have jobs that keep other people safe. Police officers and fire fighters work to help people follow rules and keep out of danger.

Did You Know?

A lifeguard at the swimming pool or beach is trained to keep people safe in the water.

7

Doctors and nurses and *ambulance* drivers all work to help other people stay healthy. Doctors and nurses go to school for a long time to learn their *skills*.

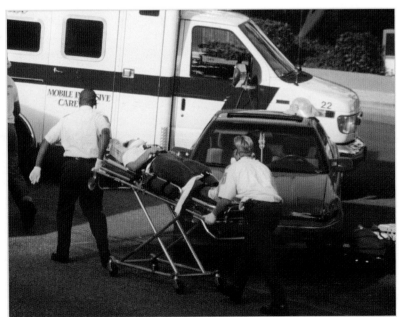

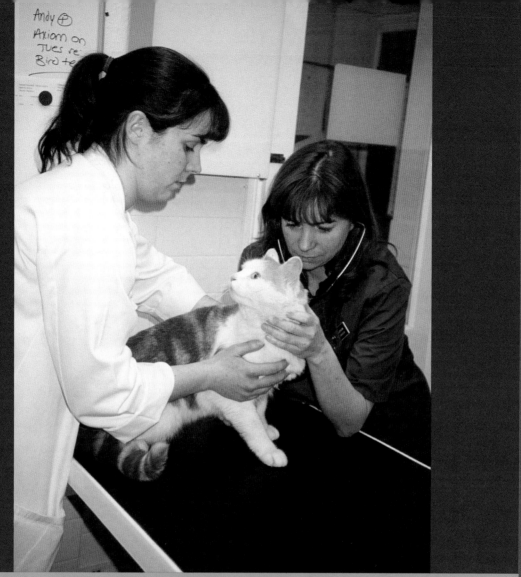

Did You Know?

Animal doctors are called veterinarians. They have to know how to take care of many kinds of animals.

When you go on vacation, almost everyone you meet is doing a service job. People who work in hotels, airports, and restaurants are there to make sure you have a good time.

Did You Know?

When people eat in restaurants, they usually leave their waiter or waitress a *tip* as a thank you for good service.

People who travel into space and people who study the deepest oceans have scientific jobs. A biologist studies living plants and animals. A geologist studies Earth's rocks.

Did You Know?

If a person's job title ends in "ist," such as a biologist, that person probably has a scientific job.

Open a newspaper or turn on a television to see news or entertainment. News people tell what is happening in the world. Actors perform to entertain people.

Did You Know?

Before television, people listened to their favorite shows on the radio.

Factory workers and construction workers are people who work to build things. In fact, most of the things you use every day were built by people somewhere.

An architect is a person who plans what a building will look like.

Different Jobs

There are many other kinds of jobs. Some people work from home on computers. Some people *travel* with their jobs and are not home very much.

What kind of job would you like to do?

Did You Know?

Most people change their jobs four or five times during their lives.

Odd Jobs

There are people called hand models. Their job is to make sure their hands look nice for commercials or **advertisements**.

Plants are people who are paid to laugh very loud while they watch the taping of a television show.

20

Did you know that people get paid to make sure that reclining chairs are comfortable?

Some people have jobs giving pets *massages*. They do this to help pets heal if they get hurt.

Glossary

advertisement–pictures and words that try to get people to buy something

ambulance–a truck or van that carries sick people to the hospital

massage–to rub skin and muscles to help them feel better

skill–a special thing a person can do after lots of training and practice

tip–extra money people leave for a waiter or waitress

travel–to leave home and go to a different place

Books

Gibson, Karen. *Truck Drivers*. Mankato, Minn.: Bridgestone Books, 2001.

Schaefer, Lola M. *We Need Fire Fighters*. Mankato, Minn.: Pebble Books, 2000.

Schaefer, Lola M. *We Need Nurses*. Mankato, Minn.: Pebble Books, 2000.

Web Sites

pbskids.org/arthur/grownups/ activities/play_learn1/when_i.html

www.talktothevet.com/KIDS/index.html

Index

GR: H

Word Count: 232

From David Conrad

I am a scientist who lives in Colorado. I like to climb mountains, square dance, and play with my pet frog, Clyde.

24